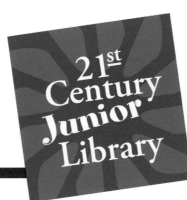

21st Century Junior Library

FARM ANIMALS
TURKEYS

by Katie Marsico

CHERRY LAKE PUBLISHING * ANN ARBOR, MICHIGAN

Published in the United States of America by Cherry Lake Publishing
Ann Arbor, Michigan
www.cherrylakepublishing.com

Content Adviser: Bev Pounds, Pounds Turkey Farm, Leechburg, Pennsylvania
Reading Adviser: Cecilia Minden-Cupp, PhD, Literacy Consultant

Photo Credits: Cover: ©Volokhatiuk/Dreamstime.com, ©Joy Brown/Shutterstock, Inc., ©Jovan Nikolic/
Shutterstock, Inc., ©Nigel Paul Monckton/Shutterstock, Inc.; page 4, ©msheldrake/Shutterstock, Inc.;
pages 6, 8, 10, 12, 14, and 18, ©J.P. Crissman; page 16, ©iStockphoto.com/DNY59; page 20,
©Rmarmion/Dreamstime.com

LIBRARY OF CONGRESS CATALOGING-IN-PUBLICATION DATA
Marsico, Katie, 1980–
 Farm animals: turkeys/by Katie Marsico.
     p. cm.—(21st century junior library)
 Includes bibliographical references and index.
 Audience: K to grade 3.
 ISBN-13: 978-1-60279-976-9 (lib. bdg.)
 ISBN-10: 1-60279-976-8 (lib. bdg.)
 1. Turkeys—Juvenile literature. I. Title. II. Title: Turkeys. III. Series: 21st century junior library.
 SF507.M387 2011
 636.5'92—dc22   2010029537

Cherry Lake Publishing would like to acknowledge the work of
The Partnership for 21st Century Skills.
Please visit www.21stcenturyskills.org *for more information.*

Printed in the United States of America
Corporate Graphics Inc.
January 2011
CLSP08

CONTENTS

Roast turkey is often served at
Thanksgiving dinner.

Thanksgiving Dinner

What does your family eat on Thanksgiving? Many people eat turkey. Turkey meat tastes great. Most turkeys are raised on turkey farms. Let's learn more about these birds.

It takes about 28 days for a turkey egg to hatch.

Gobble, Gobble, Gobble

Did someone say, "Gobble, gobble, gobble"? Male turkeys make this sound. Adult male turkeys are called **toms**. Adult females are called **hens**.

Farm hens can lay 80 to 100 eggs in just 25 weeks. Baby turkeys are called **poults**. They hatch from the eggs.

Turkeys don't have feathers on their heads.

How big do farm turkeys get? Adults weigh between 15 and 33 pounds (7 and 15 kilograms). Then they are ready to be sold. Most farm turkeys are too heavy to fly.

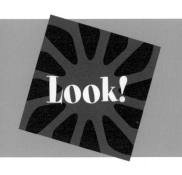

Look!

Turkeys have white or brown feathers. Their heads are bald. A piece of skin called a **snood** hangs over a turkey's beak. Another flap of skin called a **wattle** hangs under the turkey's beak.

Some farmers keep their turkeys in small buildings.

Let's Look at Turkey Farms!

There are different kinds of turkey farms. Owners of some farms raise turkeys from eggs to adults. Not all turkey farms work this way though.

Farmers make sure that their turkeys have food to eat.

Some farmers work at **hatcheries**.
Those are places where hens lay a lot of
eggs. After the eggs hatch, the poults are
sold to other farms. Farmers there raise the
poults until they are adults. They are ready
to be sold for meat when they are 16 to
24 weeks old.

Think!

Turkey farmers have many jobs. They need to
provide the turkeys with enough **feed** to eat. The birds
also need fresh water to drink. What other chores
do you think turkey farmers have? Who cleans the
turkey **coops**?

Farmers should make sure their turkeys get plenty of fresh air and sunshine.

Farm turkeys live together in big coops. This gives them room to move around. The turkeys can also get a lot of fresh air and sunshine.

Do you like to eat turkey?

Important Turkey Products

Turkey meat is tasty. It is full of **protein**. Protein gives us energy. It helps our bodies grow and stay strong. People also like turkey meat because it is **lean**. Lean meat is good for our bodies. It has very little fat.

What can turkey feathers be used for?

Most farmers raise turkeys for meat. These birds have other uses, too.

Turkey feathers are used as food for other farm animals. Sometimes feathers are ground up and used in **fertilizer**. Parts of the feathers can also be used to make yarn. Turkey droppings can be used as fertilizer or **fuel**.

Turkey can be a tasty part of any dinner.

What is the most important product to come from a turkey farm? You might say that the tastiest one is your Thanksgiving dinner!

Ask Questions!

Ask your parents what turkey products they buy. What turkey dishes do they cook? Asking questions is a great way to learn!

GLOSSARY

coops (KOOPS) buildings or outdoor areas where turkeys are kept

feed (FEED) grains and seeds that are fed to farm turkeys

fertilizer (FUHR-tuh-lye-zuhr) a substance used to make soil better for growing plants

fuel (FYOOL) a substance that can be burned to produce energy

hatcheries (HA-chuh-reez) farms where farmers raise eggs and poults

hens (HENZ) adult female turkeys

lean (LEEN) low in fat

poults (POLTZ) baby turkeys

protein (PRO-teen) a substance that helps the human body grow and stay strong

snood (SNOOD) a piece of skin that hangs over a turkey's beak

toms (TOMZ) adult male turkeys

wattle (WAT-uhl) loose skin under a turkey's beak

FIND OUT MORE

BOOKS

Endres, Hollie J. *Turkeys*. Minneapolis: Bellwether Media, 2008.

Stockland, Patricia M. *In the Turkey Pen*. Edina, MN: Magic Wagon, 2010.

WEB SITES

KidsFarm: Turkeys
www.kidsfarm.com/turkeys.htm
Listen to some of the noises that turkeys make.

KidZone: The American Turkey
www.kidzone.ws/animals/turkey.htm
Learn more fun facts about both wild and farm turkeys.

INDEX

ABOUT THE AUTHOR

Katie Marsico has written more than 60 books for young readers. She dedicates this book to her mother, Ann; mother-in-law, Bonnie; brother-in-law Jaime; and Aunt Joan. They are all expert chefs when it comes to cooking turkey.